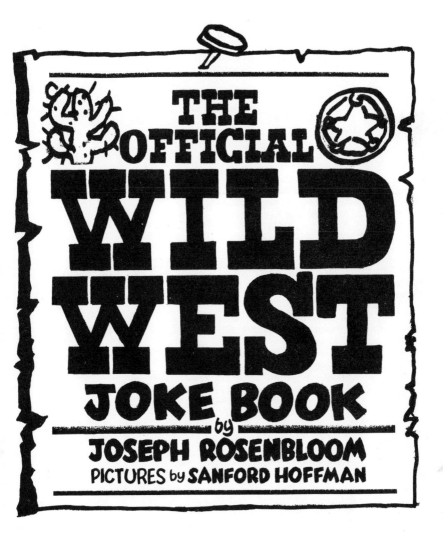

THE OFFICIAL WILD WEST JOKE BOOK

by
JOSEPH ROSENBLOOM

PICTURES by **SANFORD HOFFMAN**

Sterling Publishing Co., Inc. New York

Distributed in the U.K. by Blandford Press

Also by Joseph Rosenbloom

Bananas Don't Grow on Trees
Biggest Riddle Book in the World
Daffy Definitions
Doctor Knock-Knock's Official Knock-Knock Dictionary
Funny Insults & Snappy Put-Downs
Gigantic Joke Book
How Do You Make an Elephant Laugh?
Looniest Limerick Book in the World
Mad Scientist
Monster Madness
Polar Bears Like It Hot
Ridiculous Nicholas Pet Riddles
Ridiculous Nicholas Riddle Book
Silly Verse (and Even Worse)

Library of Congress Cataloging in Publication Data

Rosenbloom, Joseph.
    The official Wild West joke book.

    Includes index.
    Summary: Jokes, riddles, tongue twisters, and
other humor with an Old West theme.
    1. Frontier and pioneer life—West (U.S.)—
Anecdotes, facetiae, satire, etc.   2. West (U.S.)—
History—Anecdotes, facetiae, satire, etc.   3. Wit and
humor, Juvenile.   [1. Frontier and pioneer life—West
(U.S.)—Wit and humor.   2. West (U.S.)—Wit and humor.
3. Jokes]   I. Hoffman, Sanford, ill.   II. Title

PN6231.W4R67   1983   818'.5402   82-19537
ISBN 0-8069-4666-0
ISBN 0-8069-4667-9 (lib. bdg.)

Contents

To David and Sandy Backerman

1

Howdy, Partner

Where do cattle go for entertainment?
To the mooovies.

Which newspaper do cattle read?
The Daily Moos.

"Look at that bunch of cattle."
    "Not bunch of cattle—herd."
"Heard what?"
    "Of cattle."
"Sure, I've heard of cattle."
    "No, I mean cattle herd."
"So what? I've no secrets from them."

The Sheriff found an egg in the middle of Dodge City. Where did it come from?
From a chicken.

Why did the Sheriff arrest the chicken?
It used fowl language.

What kind of pole do you have when five frogs sit on top of each other?
A toad-em pole.

What has four legs and can see just as well from either end?
A horse with its eyes closed.

Where do you send a sick pony?
To the horsepital.

CLEM: I lost my horse.
LEM: Why don't you put an ad in the paper?
CLEM: What good would that do? My horse can't read.

Why did the cowboy ride tall in the saddle?
Too many saddle sores.

What is a sheep's favorite snack?
A bah-loney sandwich.

Why are sheep poor?
Because they're always being fleeced.

What does a male sheep do when he gets angry?
He goes on a ram-page.

Who is the meanest goat in the West?
Billy the Kid.

How are goats impolite?
They're always butting in.

What do you call an undersized goat?
A peanut butt-er.

What would you have if a young goat fell
into a blender?
A mixed-up kid.

Two cowboys were out on the range,
sitting around a campfire, when a huge
grizzly bear suddenly appeared in front of
them.

"Keep calm," said the first cowboy.
"Remember what we read in that book. If
you stay absolutely still and look the bear
straight in the eye, he won't attack you."

"I don't know about that," said the
second cowboy. "You've read the book,
and I've read the book—but has the bear
read the book?"

What happened when the goat ate the candle?

It burped with delight (the light).

How do you spell an Indian tent with only two letters?

T P.

Who lived in a TP?

An N D N.

What kind of hawk has no wings?

A toma-hawk.

What do you get if you cross a Hawaiian dancer and an Indian brave?

A hula-whoop.

How did the Indians get to be the first people in North America?

They had reservations.

If a posse of ten men chased one outlaw, what time would it be?

Ten after one.

Why did the Sheriff arrest the clock?
Because it struck twelve.

Why did the Sheriff arrest the walls?
For holding up the ceiling.

Why did the Sheriff arrest the pair of watches he found in the mud?
Because they were a couple of dirty two-timers.

What did the banana do when it saw Billy the Kid?
The banana split.

How did the Masked Banana escape the posse?
It gave them the slip.

What is small and yellow and wears a mask?
The Lone Lemon.

How do you make a strawberry shake?
Introduce it to Jesse James.

2

Smile When You Say That

JUDGE: I must charge you with murder.
OUTLAW: Okay, what do I owe you?

DEPUTY: What's the new prisoner like?
SHERIFF: He's mean, low, nasty, dirty,
    rotten . . . and those are just his good
    points.

What kind of play do prisoners like to put
on?
    A cell-out (sell-out).

Why did the Sheriff arrest the stale loaf of bread?

It tried to get fresh.

Why did the Sheriff put the deck of cards behind bars?

The joker was wild.

When is a jail not on land and not on water?

When it is on fire.

SHERIFF: Deputy! Deputy! Where are you?
DEPUTY: I'm here, hiding in the closet.
SHERIFF: But what are you doing in the closet?
DEPUTY: You told me to read *Dr. Jekyll and Hyde*.

DEPUTY: I had a watch stolen from under my nose last night.
SHERIFF: Well, that's a funny place to wear it.

What did the boots say to the cowboy?
"You ride. I'll go on foot."

DEPUTY: Ouch! My new boots hurt when I step on them.

SHERIFF: No wonder! You have them on the wrong feet.

DEPUTY: But I don't have any other feet!

If a cow could talk, what would it say?
Udder nonsense.

What would you have if a masked outlaw were run over by stampeding cattle?
The Mashed Bandit.

What would you have if Batman and Robin were run over by stampeding cattle?
Flatman and Ribbon.

Why did the Sheriff use a ruler when he questioned the witness?
He wanted to get the story straight.

CLEM: Did you hear the one about the outlaw who stole a rooster and a steer?

LEM: No, what about it?

CLEM: Never mind, it's a cock-and-bull story.

What would you get if you crossed a chicken and a cow?

Roost beef.

SHERIFF: How could you let the outlaw escape?

DEPUTY: I couldn't help it, Sheriff. He stepped on a scale and got a weigh.

What has two arms, two wings, two tails, three heads, three bodies and eight legs?

A cowboy on horseback holding a chicken.

Why did the muddy chicken cross the road twice?

Because it was a dirty double crosser.

SHERIFF: The outlaw got away, eh? Didn't you guard the exits like I told you?

DEPUTY: Yes, I did, Sheriff. But the outlaw tricked me. He went out through the entrance.

SHERIFF: *(standing over the body of an outlaw named Juan):* He must have been shot with a golf gun.

DEPUTY: What's a golf gun?

SHERIFF: The gun that made a hole in Juan (hole in one).

SHERIFF: What would you do if you found a million dollars?

DEPUTY: Well, if it was a poor person who lost it, I'd return it.

What does a pickle say when it wants to enter a poker game?

"Dill me in."

What is the hardest thing to deal with in a poker game?

A greasy deck of cards.

PRISONER: Why don't you play checkers with the Sheriff anymore?

DEPUTY: Would you play with a guy who cheats and moves his men around when you're not looking?

PRISONER: No, I wouldn't.

DEPUTY: Well—neither would he.

FIRST COWBOY: You play checkers with your dog? He must be pretty smart.

SECOND COWBOY: Not really. I beat him most of the time.

A little girl from the city, seeing a horse being shod, rushed to her mother.

"Mommy," she cried, "there's a man out there building a horse. I just saw him nailing on the feet!"

Why don't cowboys ever play hide-and-seek near a mountain?
Because the mountain peaks.

What musical note do you hear when a horse falls on a man who's digging for gold?
A-flat minor.

What would you have if cattle fought each other?
Steer Wars.

How do cowboys drive steers?
With steer-ing wheels.

CLEM: Did you hear the story about the branding iron?
LEM: No, what about it?
CLEM: Never mind, it's too hot to handle.

What do you get if you cross a branding iron and the top of an iceberg?
A hot tip.

Why was the bowlegged cowboy fired?
Because he couldn't get his calves together.

3

Quick on the Draw

What is small, purple and dangerous?
A grape with a six-shooter.

When is a gun unemployed?
When it is fired.

What is a shot gun?
A worn-out rifle.

What kind of cat does a wounded cowboy look for?
A first-aid kit.

How come a duck won the sharpshooting contest?
He was a quack shot.

What lives in the ocean, has eight legs and is quick on the draw?
Billy the Squid.

What's the difference between a six-shooter and a toothpick?
If you don't know, better not pick your teeth.

What do you call a baby rifle?
A son-of-a-gun.

SHERIFF: Can you hit that circle with your rifle?

DEPUTY: No, I'm a square shooter.

SHERIFF: I just met a cowboy who is so dumb he thinks a football coach has four wheels.

DEPUTY: How many wheels does it have?

Why did the cowboy carry a cannon into town?

He wanted people to think he was a big shot.

SHERIFF: How many shots did the outlaw fire at you?

DEPUTY: I counted two shots—definitely. One when the bullet passed me, and one when I passed the bullet.

Why did the sharpshooter carry a ruler?
So he could shoot straight.

What is the difference between a sharpshooter and chocolate cake?
One hits the mark; the other hits the spot.

CLEM: Why did the cowboy aim his gun at the fan?

LEM: He was just shooting the breeze.

SHERIFF: If you had a gun with only one bullet, and one outlaw was coming at you from one direction and another outlaw from another direction, which would you shoot?

DEPUTY: I'd shoot the gun.

When is a pistol like a young horse?
When it is a Colt.

BIFF: What is the difference between a roll and a six-shooter?
CLIFF: I don't know.
BIFF: Well, if you don't know, remind me not to send you out for hamburgers.

How do people feel after they're shot by a six-shooter?
Holier.

SAY THESE 3 TIMES QUICKLY

Sharpshooters should shoot slowly.

Sixty-six sick six-shooters.

"The sharpshooters are shipshape, sir."

A genuine judge just judges justly.

Good gunsmoke—bad gunsmoke.

Six cattle slip on slick ski slopes.

No stagecoach stops at Smith's fresh fish-sauce shop.

OUTLAW: KNOCK, KNOCK!
STAGECOACH DRIVER: Who's there?
OUTLAW: Dick.
STAGECOACH DRIVER: Dick who?
OUTLAW: Dick 'em up!

OUTLAW: KNOCK, KNOCK!
STAGECOACH DRIVER: Who's there?
OUTLAW: Hanover.
STAGECOACH DRIVER: Hanover who?
OUTLAW: Hanover your money.

OUTLAW: KNOCK, KNOCK!
STAGECOACH DRIVER: Who's there?
OUTLAW: Ferdie
STAGECOACH DRIVER: Ferdie who?
OUTLAW: Ferdie last time, hand over your money!

STAGECOACH DRIVER: KNOCK, KNOCK!
OUTLAW: Who's there?
STAGECOACH DRIVER: Doughnut.
OUTLAW: Doughnut who?
STAGECOACH DRIVER: Doughnut shoot!
I give up.

Why is a stolen pistol like a racing car?
They're both hot rods.

A Texas lad rushed home from kindergarten and insisted that his mother buy him a set of pencils, a gun belt and a pair of six-shooters.

"Whatever for, dear?" his mother asked. "You're not going to tell me you need them for school?"

"Yes, I do," he replied. "Teacher said that tomorrow she's going to teach me how to draw."

BIFF: I got fired from my job as bank guard today.

CLIFF: How come?

BIFF: A masked bandit came into the bank. I drew my gun and told him that if he took one more step, I'd let him have it.

CLIFF: What did he do?

BIFF: He took one more step, so I let him have it. Who wanted that dumb old gun, anyway?

4

You Got Me!

What is the difference between a jeweler and a jailer?

A jeweler sells watches; a jailer watches cells.

JUDGE: You look familiar. Have you ever been up before me?

OUTLAW: I don't know. What time do you get up?

When is a football player like a judge?
When he's on the bench.

How are judges like tennis players?
Both work the courts.

PRISONER *(to Judge)*: What floor are we
   on, Your Honor?
JUDGE: The second floor.
PRISONER: I'm going upstairs.
JUDGE: What for?
PRISONER: I want to take my case to a
   higher court.

What kind of candy would a doomed
prisoner like to have before he is hanged?
A Life Saver.

What did the prisoner about to be hanged say when he was pardoned at the last minute?

"No noose is good noose."

What hired killer never goes to jail?

An exterminator.

What is the favorite sport of executioners?

Hang gliding.

What did the hangman give his wife for her birthday?

A choker.

How do hangmen keep up with current events?

They read the noose-paper.

When an executioner checked in at a hotel, the clerk asked him what kind of room he wanted. "A small one," he replied. "I just need a place to hang my hat and a few friends."

What kind of party do prisoners like best?

A going-away party.

Why did the prisoner eat a lot of sweets?

He was hoping to break out.

An outlaw was in jail. All he had in his cell was a piano. Yet, he managed to escape. How did he do it?

He played the piano until he found the right key.

How is an escaping prisoner like an airline pilot?

Both want safe flights.

How are prisoners like astronauts?

Both are interested in outer space.

What did the picture say to the Sheriff?
"I've been framed!"

SCHOOLTEACHER*(visiting the jail):* What are
   you doing?
PRISONER: I'm sawing the bars.
SCHOOLTEACHER: Tut, tut, where's your
   grammar? You should say, "I'm
   seeing the bars!"

A prisoner escaped from jail and said to a
little boy he met, "Hooray! I'm free! I'm
free!"

"So what!" replied the little boy. "I'm
four!"

What is green and has two legs and a trunk?

A stagecoach passenger with motion sickness.

FIRST OLD-TIMER: Is it true that the actor was hit by a Wells Fargo wagon?

SECOND OLD-TIMER: Yep, poor feller's been stage struck ever since.

JUDGE: The next person who raises his
　　　voice in this court will be thrown out.
PRISONER: Hip, hip, hooray! Hip, hip,
　　　hooray!

JUDGE: Order! Order in the court!
OUTLAW: I'll have a hamburger on a roll
　　　with mustard and a Coke, please.

CLEM: What happened to the outlaw who
　　　stole the watch?
LEM: The lawyer got the case and the
　　　judge gave him time.

Why did the Sheriff arrest the clothespins?

For holding up a pair of pants.

Why did the Sheriff arrest the tennis players?

Because they had racquets.

What was the Sheriff doing in the shoe store?

Rounding up all the sneakers and the loafers.

Why did the outlaw take a shower before he broke out of jail?

He wanted to make a clean getaway.

How many outlaws can you put into an empty cell?

One. After that the cell isn't empty anymore.

Why are outlaws in jail the slowest talkers in the world?

They can spend 25 years on a single sentence.

5

He Went That-a-Way

FIRST OLD-TIMER: Did you see the varmint
that stole the computer?
SECOND OLD-TIMER: Yep, he went data-way!

What is green and dangerous?
A thundering herd of pickles.

Who is the toughest pickle in Dodge City?
Marshall Dill.

Why did the Sheriff go to the barbecue?
*He heard it was a place to have a
steak out.*

Why did the Sheriff arrest the fisherman?
For packing a rod.

Why did the Sheriff arrest the cook?
For beating the eggs and whipping the cream.

Why did the Sheriff arrest the photographer?
He shot his customers and then blew them up.

Why couldn't the Sheriff keep a clock in jail?

Because time was always running out.

What do you get if you cross a clock and a gun?

A ticks-shooter.

Why did Jesse James shoot the clock?
He wanted to kill time.

What would happen if an ice cream cone picked a fight with Jesse James?

The ice cream cone would get licked.

What do you call Jesse James when he has the flu?

A sick shooter.

What would you get if you crossed Jesse James and a cow?

Better not try it. Jesse James doesn't like to be crossed.

Who robbed stagecoaches and wore dirty clothes?

Messy James.

DEPUTY: Are you really going to take the stagecoach out in weather like this?

STAGECOACH DRIVER: It's driving rain, isn't it?

Why did the outlaw carry a bottle of glue when he robbed the stagecoach?

So he could stick up the passengers.

Why is a Wells Fargo driver like a person who works in the theatre?

Both are stage managers.

FIRST COWBOY: Did you hear the big noise this morning?

SECOND COWBOY: No, what was it—the crack of dawn?

FIRST COWBOY: Nope, it was the break of day.

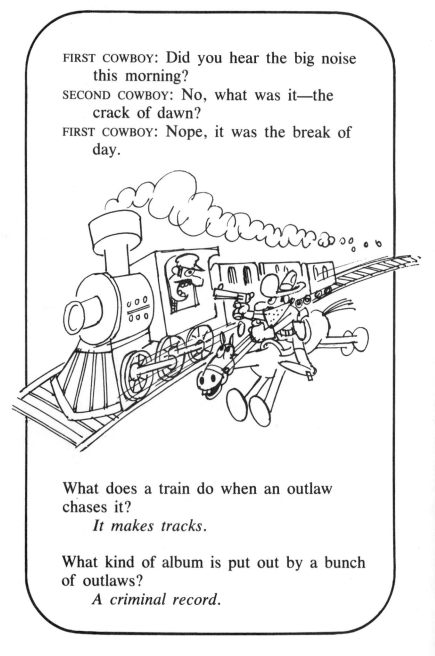

What does a train do when an outlaw chases it?
It makes tracks.

What kind of album is put out by a bunch of outlaws?
A criminal record.

JUDGE: Have you ever held up trains?
OUTLAW: Now and then.
JUDGE: Where have you held up trains?
OUTLAW: Here and there.
JUDGE: What things have you taken from the passengers?
OUTLAW: This and that.
JUDGE: Sheriff, lock this man up!
OUTLAW: Hey! When do I get out of jail?
JUDGE: Oh—sooner or later.

What is more frightening than one mean outlaw?

Two mean outlaws.

What kind of band seldom makes music?
An outlaw band.

A horse walked into a saloon and ordered a beer. He drank up, smacked his lips and paid. Then he left without saying another word.

"Wow, a talking horse!" exclaimed a cowboy to the bartender.

"We don't pay him much mind," said the bartender. "He never even says good night."

SHERIFF: How could you let the robber get away from you in broad daylight?

DEPUTY: I couldn't help it, Sheriff. He ran into a movie theatre.

SHERIFF: Why didn't you run in after him?

DEPUTY: I would have, but I already saw the movie.

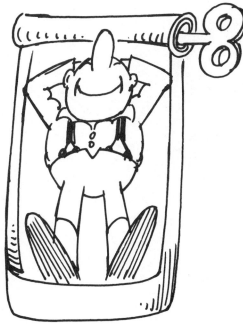

COWBOY (*boasting*): Out on the range I can live for a week on a can of sardines.

CITY MAN: How do you keep from falling off?

How is a bank like a herd of deer?
You can always find a buck in it.

What would you get if you crossed Jesse James and Count Dracula?
A robbery at the blood bank.

Why is it hard to keep a bank robbery secret?
Because so many people who work in the bank are tellers.

If a millionaire sits on gold, who sits on Silver?

The Lone Ranger.

What has a point on one end, a feather on the other end, and goes "Click, click, click?"

A ball-point arrow.

When is an artist like an Indian with an arrow?

When he draws a bow.

Why did the banana run from the outlaw?
Because it was yellow.

Two cowhands were riding on a train
for the first time. They had brought along
bananas to eat on the trip. Just as they
began to peel the bananas, the train
entered a dark tunnel.

"Have you eaten your banana yet?" the
first cowhand cried.

"No," replied the second cowhand.

"Well, don't touch it!" warned the first
cowhand. "I took one bite and went
blind!"

A cowboy walking along the road saw an
Indian lying with his ear to the ground,
mumbling. He went over and listened. The
Indian said, "Stagecoach, spoked wheels,
green and yellow, four horses, driver with
red hair."

The cowboy was astonished. "Do you
mean you can tell all that by just listening
with your ear to the ground?"

"Ear to the ground nothing!" the Indian
replied. "That stagecoach ran over me!"

6

Inlaws and Outlaws

What did the outlaw get for holding up the rubber band factory?

A long stretch.

What did the outlaw get for stealing the calendar?

Twelve months.

What happened to the outlaw who fell into the cement mixer?

He became a hardened criminal.

What happened when the outlaws and the posse jumped out of the plane?

They had a chute out.

What happened when the outlaw ran away with the circus?

The Sheriff made him bring it back.

Why did the outlaw gang try to steal the baseball field?

Because it was the biggest diamond in the world.

Why did the outlaw try to steal the dictionary?

He heard there was "money" in it.

Two outlaws robbed a bank. They decided to bury the money they stole. If it took two outlaws five days to dig a hole, how many days would it take them to dig half a hole?

None. You can't dig half a hole.

How do you treat an outlaw with an itchy trigger finger?

With respect.

What is better than presence of mind when you meet an outlaw gang?
Absence of body.

What is the safest way to talk to an outlaw?
By long distance.

What do you call an outlaw with cotton stuffed in his ears?
Anything you want. He can't hear you.

What did the victim say when the outlaw stuffed a dirty piece of cloth in his mouth?

"That's an old gag."

DEPUTY: Are you going to the big execution today?

SHERIFF: No, where is it?

DEPUTY: At the art gallery. They're going to hang a bunch of pictures.

What happened when the painter threw his pictures at the outlaw?

The outlaw had an art attack.

Why did the outlaw hold up the river?
He heard it had two banks.

Why did the outlaw hold up air-conditioned banks?
To get cold cash.

Why did the outlaw steal the deck of cards?
He heard there were 13 diamonds in it.

Why did the outlaw hold up the bakery?
He kneaded the dough.

Why did the gang of outlaws suddenly leave the restaurant?
Because they had finished eating.

Why can't an outlaw living in Texas be buried in Oklahoma?
Because he's still living!

Why was the outlaw buried in the town cemetery?
Because he was dead.

Why is pollution like a crime?
It is a great terrain robbery.

What kind of outlaws wear suspenders?
Hold-up men.

What is an outlaw's favorite bird?
The robin.

A Cub Scout troop visited the Sheriff's office and saw pictures of "wanted" outlaws on the wall. One little boy pointed to a picture and asked if that really was the photograph of the wanted outlaw. The Sheriff said it was. "Then why," asked the little boy, "didn't you keep him when you took his picture?"

What kind of outlaw steals soap and towels?
   A dirty crook.

When is an outlaw neither left-handed nor right-handed?

When he is underhanded.

What is the difference between an outlaw and a church bell?

One steals from the people; the other peals from the steeple.

What do outlaws eat with their milk?

Crookies.

What kind of sweets do outlaws steal?

Hot chocolate.

What happened when the outlaw swallowed his knife and fork?

He had to eat with his hands.

What do you get if you cross a big bell and an outlaw?

A gongster.

What do you get if an outlaw band falls into the ocean?

A crime wave.

TOM: What do you say to an outlaw when he aims his rifle at you?

JERRY: I give up.

TOM: Right! Only you say it faster.

What do you call a short, sunburned outlaw riding a horse?
> *Little Red Riding Hood.*

What kind of bars won't keep an outlaw in jail?
> *Chocolate bars.*

CLEM: Dangerous outlaws make people smaller?
LEM: Sure—don't people shrink from them?

What kind of bandit steals from cats?
> *A purr-snatcher.*

OUTLAW: This is a stick-up. Give me your money or else. . . .
VICTIM: Or else what?
OUTLAW: Don't get me confused. This is my first job.

What did the outlaw say to the leaking dam?
> *"One more crack and I'll plug you!"*

CLEM: Did you hear about the outlaw who was put in jail for stealing a pig?
LEM: How did they catch him?
CLEM: The pig squealed.

7

Ride 'Em, Cowboy!

KNOCK KNOCK!
Who's there?
You.
You who?
Ride 'em, cowboy!

What do you get if you tickle a fat cowboy's stomach?
Belly laughs.

Why did the cowboy put up his tent on the stove?
So he could have a home on the range.

When is a cowboy most like a pony?
When he is a little hoarse.

Why do cowboys ride horses?
Because the horses are too heavy to carry.

Why did the cowboy saddle up a porcupine?
So he wouldn't have to ride it bareback.

Why did the cowboy brush his teeth with gunpowder?

So he could shoot his mouth off.

Why did the cowboy put a whistle in his ten-gallon hat?

In case he wanted to blow his top.

What happened after the cowboy drank eight Cokes?

He burped 7-Up.

What song do bored cowboys sing?
"Ho-hum on the Range."

Why did the cowboy buy a dachshund?
Because his favorite song was "Get Along Little Dogie."

What kind of music did the cowboy make when he threw a stone in the Rio Grande?
Plunk rock.

Why did the cowboy saddle up the phonograph record?

He wanted to be a disc jockey.

How do cowboys watch TV when they're out on the range?

By communication saddle lights (satellites).

What does a cowboy say to his horse after a 100-mile ride?

"Whoa!"

What part of a cowboy's outfit is the saddest?

Blue jeans.

CLEM: Did you hear about the 12-foot-long bed?

LEM: No, what about it?

CLEM: Never mind, it's a lot of bunk.

Why did the cowboy put his bunk in the fireplace?

So he could sleep like a log.

Why did the cowboy run around his bunk?

So he could catch up on his sleep.

How does a cowboy get through a patch of poison ivy?
He itch hikes.

What do you call a sleeping bull?
A bull dozer.

DEPUTY: I hear that a charging bull won't hurt you if you carry a flashlight.
SHERIFF: True—if you carry it fast enough.

A rancher walked up to the window at the post office where a new clerk was sorting mail.

"Any mail for Mike Howe?" the rancher asked.

The clerk ignored him, and the rancher repeated his question in a louder voice. Without looking up, the clerk said, "No, none for your cow, and none for your horse, either."

SONG (*Sung to the Tune of "Home on the Range"*)
Oh, give me a home
Where the buffalo roam,
And the cowboys—they work till they drop,
Where the cows all relax
Lying flat on their backs,
And this brings the cream to the top.

What did the cowboy say when he backed into the cactus?
"Ouch!"

Why did the cowboy ignore the "Danger" sign on the cliff?
Because he thought it was only a bluff.

What do you call a cowboy who sticks his right arm down the mouth of a mountain lion?
"Lefty."

The cowboy strode into the restaurant yelling, "All right, all right, who is the wise guy who painted my horse yellow?" There was a silence in the restaurant. "Show yourself, if you dare!" shouted the cowboy.

A 7-foot tall, mean-looking character got up from a table and rested his hands on his gun handles. "I did it," he said coolly. "What did you want to tell me?"

The cowboy swallowed hard. "I thought you'd like to know," he said, "the first coat is dry."

What kind of cowboy never lets anything get in his hair?
A bald one.

Why did the cowboy wear loud socks?
So his foot wouldn't fall asleep.

Where do most of the nuts in Dodge City hang out?
At the Hershey bar.

Where do dead cowboys go on Saturday night?
To ghost towns.

Which cowboy wears the biggest boots?
The one with the biggest feet.

Where do cowboys send their shoes
during the summer months?
To boot camp.

Did you hear about the cowboy who was
so stupid that when he saw a sign saying
"Man Wanted for Robbery," he applied
for the job?

BEST SELLER LIST

1. *Riding Wild Stallions* by Eiffel Downe and Aiken Backe

2. *My Life As an Outlaw* by I. Ben Bad

3. *How to Become a Successful Outlaw* by Robin Steele

4. *Cowboy Cooking Simplified* by Frank N. Beans and Chuck Wagon

5. *Time for Chow* by Dean R. Bell

6. *Getting Around in the Old Days* by Horace N. Buggy

7. *Breaking Out of Jail* by S. Kape

8. *Guide to Playing Poker* by Delia Cards

9. *Donkeys in the West* by Jack Cass

10. *Popular Cowboy Songs* by Mel O. Dee

Why did the little goat run away from home?

It wanted to join the Goats Guard.

RANCHER: You want to work around here?
Can you shoe horses?
COWHAND: No, but I can shoe flies.

What kind of ponchos do Mexican
cowboys wear on a rainy day?
Wet ones.

Why did the cowboy take a hammer to
bed with him?
So he could hit the hay.

There were three tomatoes on a shelf.
Two were ripe and one was green. Which
one is the cowboy?
*The green one. The other two are
redskins.*

What do you do with a green cowboy?
Wait until he ripens.

What happened to the cowboy who fell
down the well?
He kicked the bucket.

8

Meanwhile Back
at the Ranch

BIFF: What's the name of your ranch?

CLIFF: The ABCDEFGHIJKLMNOP-
QRSTUVWXYZ Ranch.

BIFF: How many head of cattle do you have?

CLIFF: Not many.

BIFF: How come?

CLIFF: Not many survive the branding.

What goes all around a ranch but doesn't move?

A fence.

When is it good manners to spit in a rancher's face?

When his moustache is on fire.

Why did the rancher take the cow to the vet?

Because she was so mooo-dy.

What has six legs and walks with only four?

A horse and rider.

FIRST COWBOY: Do you want to hear a dirty joke?

SECOND COWBOY: Sure.

FIRST COWBOY: A horse fell in the mud.

A city dude went to a ranch to buy a horse. He saw a beautiful pony and asked what kind it was. "That's a palomino," the rancher said.

"Well," the city dude thought for a minute, "any friend of yours is a friend of mine."

What do cows give after an earthquake?
    Milk shakes.

Where do cowboys take their sheep for a haircut?

To the bah-bah shop.

What did the cowboy say when he wanted to get the sheep's attention?

"Hey, ewe!"

If dogs have fleas, what do sheep have?

Fleece.

What kind of horses frighten ranchers?

Nightmares.

What seven letters of the alphabet did the outlaw say when he opened the bank vault and found nothing inside?

"O I C U R M T."

Why wouldn't the Sheriff handle the dictionary?

Because he heard it had dynamite in it.

What did the tenderfoot see when he fell off his horse?

An all-star show.

How did the Sheriff find the missing barber?

He combed the town.

In what kind of home does the buffalo roam?

A very dirty one.

What did the termite say when he came into the saloon?

"Is the bar tender here?"

DEPUTY: That's a mighty strange-looking dog.

SHERIFF: He's a genuine police dog.

DEPUTY: He doesn't look like any police dog I've ever seen.

SHERIFF: Of course not. He's in the secret service.

Where do young dogs sleep when they're out on the range?

In pup tents.

Why is a kindly saltine like an outlaw?
Both are safecrackers.

Why did the little snake cry?
Someone stole its rattle.

What do you get when a herd of cattle
stampedes through a vegetable garden?
Squash.

How are snobs like victims of robbery?
Both are stuck up.

A tough cowboy demanded a room at the inn.

The innkeeper said, "I have only one room left. But before I give it to you, I have to tell you that room is where the white-eyed ghost lives."

The cowboy said, "I'll take the room

because I'm not afraid of ghosts."

That night when the cowboy went to bed he heard a scary, "Booooo! I am the white-eyed ghost."

The cowboy said, "Shut up. I'm tired."

"Booooo!" the ghost said again, "I am the white-eyed ghost—"

The cowboy sat up, reached over, picked up a chair and threw it at the ghost, who disappeared. The cowboy lay down again and shut his eyes.

"Booooo," moaned the voice from the darkness, "I am the black-eyed ghost—"

What does a sheep say when it has problems?

"Where there's a wool, there's a way."

What would you get if you crossed a porcupine and a sheep?

An animal that could knit its own sweaters.

FLIP: Did you hear about the cowboy who was trampled by a flock of sheep?
FLOP: No, what happened?
FLIP: He dyed-in-the-wool.

RANCHER: Do you realize it takes three
   sheep to make one sweater?
CITY MAN: Amazing—I didn't even know
   they could knit.

What do well-behaved lambs say to their
mothers?
   "Thank ewe."

Why did the outlaw put a pistol in each
pocket of his jacket?
   He wanted a coat of arms.

An old prospector marched into an assayer's office and threw two huge nuggets on the counter. The clerk stared at them, open-mouthed. "Well," said the prospector impatiently, "don't just stand there! Assay something."

A cowboy walked into a cafe and pounded the counter for service. A horse finally came out wearing an apron. The cowboy's eyes opened wide.

"Well," said the horse, "What do you want?"

The cowboy just stood there, staring.

"What's the matter?" asked the horse. "Haven't you ever seen a talking horse before?"

"Sorry," the cowboy apologized, "I didn't know the buffalo sold the cafe."

9

Horsin' Around

How do you make a horse float?
　　*Take two scoops of ice cream, root
　　beer—and add one horse.*

What always follows a horse?
　　Its tail.

Which part of the horse is most
important?
　　The mane (main) part.

What season is it when a tenderfoot tries to ride a wild stallion?
Fall.

TENDERFOOT: How do you lead a wild stallion?
COWBOY: It's simple. First you get a rope. Then you tie it to the wild stallion.
TENDERFOOT: And then?
COWBOY: And then you find out where the wild stallion wants to go.

"I found a horseshoe—that means good luck!"

"It may mean good luck to you—but some poor horse is now running around in his stocking feet!"

What four letters of the alphabet could you say to a person who just fell off a horse?
R.U.O.K.?

When is a horse not a horse?
When it turns into a stable.

How long should a horse's legs be?
Long enough to the reach the ground.

NIT: How do you get down from a horse?
WIT: You don't get down from a horse.
You get down from a duck.

Why is a rodeo horse rich?
It has a million bucks.

What is the hardest thing about learning
to ride a bucking horse?
The ground.

How much do you have to know to teach
a horse tricks?
More than the horse.

A horse walked into a restaurant and ordered a well-done cheeseburger with onions, pickle, relish, ketchup and mustard.

The waiter brought the food to the horse, who finished it off with great pleasure.

Noticing a cowboy staring at him as he ate, the horse said, "I suppose you think it strange that a horse should come into a restaurant and order a well-done cheeseburger with onions, pickle, relish, ketchup and mustard."

"Not really," the cowboy replied. "I like it that way myself."

What kind of horse eats and drinks with its tail?
> *They all do. No horse takes off its tail to eat or drink.*

KNOCK, KNOCK!
Who's there?
Appaloosa.
Appaloosa who?
Appaloosa my grip!

A horse came into an agent's office and said, "My act is really sensational. I can fly."

The horse then flew up to the ceiling, circled the room several times and came down in a perfect landing.

The agent was not impressed. "Okay," he said, "you do bird imitations, but what else do you do?"

Why are horses always poorly dressed?
> *Because they wear shoes but no socks.*

SHERIFF: There's a man in the circus who jumps on a horse's back, slips underneath, catches hold of his tail, and finishes on the horse's neck.

TENDERFOOT: That's nothing. I did all those things the first time I rode a horse.

FIRST TENDERFOOT: Can you ride a horse?

SECOND TENDERFOOT: Don't know. I can't stay on one long enough to find out.

What was the fastest way to ship small horses in the Old West?

By Pony Express.

A circus came to town. Its star was a horse that played classical music beautifully. A cowboy who saw the show was amazed by the performance. He asked the horse's trainer how the horse could possibly have learned to play classical music so well.

"Oh, it's nothing," the trainer replied, "he's had lessons for years."

What two garden vegetables help fight crime?
Beetman and Radish.

BEST SELLER LIST

1. *Protect Your Ranch* by Bob Dwyer

2. *I Was Held Up by Outlaws* by Terry Fried

3. *I'll Eat Anything* by Billy Gote

4. *Dirty Crooks* by Phil T. Hans and Nita Bath

5. *My Life as a Cowboy* by Rhoda Horse

6. *Crime Doesn't Pay* by Landon Jail

7. *Mountain Climbing Can Be Fun* by Ava Lanche

8. *Cowboy Yodelling* by O. Leo Layee

9. *Lawmen at Work* by Hans Zupp

10. *Indian Archery* by Beau N. Arrow

When was beef at its highest?
When the cow jumped over the moon.

"Are horses good acrobats?"
   "Yes, they can turn cartwheels."

"Are horses good artists?"
   "Yes, they can draw carriages."

FIRST LITTLE BOY: My uncle can shoot a gun faster than any man in the West. He can even shoot without taking his gun out of its holster.
SECOND LITTLE BOY: What do you call your uncle?
FIRST LITTLE BOY: "Toeless Joe."

A horse was tied to a rope six feet long. A bale of hay was eighteen feet away. The horse was hungry. How could the horse eat the hay?
   Easily. The rope wasn't tied to anything.

A cowboy rides on horseback from Dodge City to Abilene. The trip normally takes four days. He leaves Dodge City on Wednesday and arrives on the same Wednesday. How can this be?
   His horse is named Wednesday.

The horse and the cowboy were shown to their seats by the theatre usher. When the film was over, the horse applauded loudly. As the horse and the cowboy left the theatre, the usher asked, "And did your horse enjoy the movie?"

"Very much," the cowboy replied.

"Amazing!" the usher said.

"I think so, too," said the cowboy, "especially since he didn't care too much for the book."

LITTLE GIRL: I would like to buy a pony. How much do they cost?

RANCHER: Ten dollars apiece.

LITTLE GIRL: I don't want a piece. How much does a whole one cost?

What did the horse say when it finished a bale of hay?

"Well, that's the last straw!"

What did the cowboy say to the horse he hadn't seen in a long time?

"I forget your name, but your pace is familiar."

10

Best of the West

SHERIFF: How much after midnight is it?
DEPUTY: I don't know, Sheriff. My watch only goes as high as twelve.

How was sports equipment transported in the Old West?
By football coach.

What western city is named for a ghost?
Casper (Wyoming).

Who was the most famous cat in the West?
Kitty Carson.

SAY THESE 3 TIMES QUICKLY

Should sheriffs sup at cheap chop suey shops?

The selfish Sheriff should share some shellfish.

The Sheriff shot a shy thrush.

Six sheriffs seek six sick sheiks.

Where is the chief cheap sheep section?

What did the big buffalo say to the little
buffalo when it left for school?
"Bison!" (Bye, son!)

A Pony Express rider was attacked by a
mountain lion. He rode to the nearest
town and limped into the post office.
"What happened to you?" asked the
postmaster.
"I was riding along when I was attacked
by a mountain lion," the rider said.
"Fortunately, he only bit me slightly."
"Did you put anything on your leg?"
"No, he liked it plain."

Why did Billy the Kid set Dodge City on fire?

So he could be the toast of the town.

What was Billy the Kid's favorite subject in school?

Triggernometry.

Who pulled the biggest holdup in history?

Atlas—he held up the whole world.

Why do outlaws sleep on the ground after they rob a bank?

Because they want to lie low.

What do you call an outlaw armed with four loaded revolvers?
"*Sir!*"

What kind of fur do you get from outlaws?
As fur as you can get.

What kind of cat chases outlaws?
A posse cat.

Who is the thirstiest cowboy in the West?
The one who drank Canada Dry.

A cowboy visited a saloon where he saw a remarkable sight. Several cowboys were sitting around a table playing poker with a small, shaggy dog.

"What a wonderful dog," the cowboy said. "He must be very intelligent to be able to play poker with human beings."

"Not really," one of the players said. "Every time he gets a good hand, he wags his tail."

Why was the animal thrown out of the poker game?

Because it was a cheetah.

Why were outlaws the strongest men in the Old West?
They could hold up trains.

What do buffaloes celebrate every 200 years?
Their Bison-tennial.

11

The Last Roundup

What do you call a cow that has lost its calf?

De-calf-inated.

What is a calf after it is a year old?
Two years old.

Where do cows dance?
In a dis-cow-teque.

Where do cattle dance?
At the meatball.

What is the quickest way to count cows?
On a cow-culator.

What key do cattle sing in?
Beef-flat (B-flat).

What kind of automobiles do rich steers drive?
Cattle-lacs.

CLEM: Can you spell COW in thirteen letters?
LEM: *SEE O DOUBLE YOU.*

What is the easiest way to keep milk from turning sour?
Leave it in the cow.

What cattle follow you wherever you go?
Your calves.

Where do calves eat?
In calf-eterias.

Where do cattle eat?
In re-steer-rants.

Why don't cows
have money?
*Because people
milk them dry.*

What goes out
black and comes
in white?
*A black cow
in a
snowstorm.*

Who is boss
in the dairy?
The big cheese.

If a papa bull eats three bales of hay and
a baby bull eats one bale, how many
bales would a mama bull eat?
*None. There's no such thing as a
mama bull.*

How do you make meatloaf?
Send a cow to the seashore.

Why don't most cows go to college?
*Because not many graduate from high
school.*

How is a political speech like a steer?
*There's a point here and there and a
lot of bull in between.*

What do you call a cattle rustler?
A beef-thief.

Why is it better to own a cow than a bull?

Because a cow gives milk, but a bull always charges.

What is the best thing to do if a bull charges you?

Pay him.

How do you keep a bull from charging?

Take away his credit cards.

Why did the cow go to the psychiatrist?

Because it had a fodder complex.

What is the most important use for cowhide?

To keep the cow together.

DOCTOR: Ever have an accident?

COWBOY: No.

DOCTOR: Never in your whole life?

COWBOY: Well, on the last roundup, a bull charged and broke three of my ribs.

DOCTOR: Don't you call that an accident?

COWBOY: No, Doctor, the bull did it on purpose.

What did the outlaw give his wife for her birthday?

A stole.

Why do sheep go into saloons?

To look for the bah-tender.

A cowboy was leading a flock of sheep down Main Street when the Sheriff ordered him to stop.

"What's wrong?" the cowboy asked. "I was just heading my ewes into a side street."

"That's the trouble," the Sheriff replied. "No ewe turns are permitted in this town."

What did the ten-gallon hat say to the outlaws?

"I've got you covered."

As the Lone Ranger and Tonto were riding along towards the north, they spotted a war party of about 50 Apaches coming at them. They turned south, but another war party appeared. Afraid now, the Lone Ranger and Tonto turned east and met another war party of 100 braves. They turned west as their last remaining hope and saw a war party of 500.

The Lone Ranger turned to his friend and said, "Well, Tonto, this is the end. I guess we're goners."

Tonto looked back at the Lone Ranger. "What do you mean *we,* paleface?"

RANCHER (*boasting*): I've got hundreds of
    cows.
COWBOY: That's a lot of cows.
RANCHER: That's not all. I've also got
    thousands of bulls.
COWBOY: That's a lot of bull.

The cowhand was getting too old to ride
the range, so he applied for a job as a
railroad switchman.

"Now, my good man," said the station
manager, "I'm going to ask you a few
simple questions. First, what would you
do if you saw two trains approaching each
other on the same track?"

"I'd throw the lever and switch one
onto another track."

"And if the signals were jammed?"

"I'd grab a red flag and run out on the
track."

"And if the train engineer didn't see
you?"

"I'd call the Deputy Sheriff."

"The Deputy Sheriff? But what could he
do?"

"Nothing. But he sure loves to watch
train wrecks."

What did the bored cow say when she got
up in the morning?
    "Just an udder day."

Index